The Blind Child in the Regular Kindergarten

Never check the actions of the child; follow him, and watch him to prevent any serious accidents, but do not interfere unnecessarily; do not even remove obstacles which he would learn to avoid by tumbling over them a few times. . . . Do not too much regard bumps on the forehead, rough scratches or bloody noses; even these may have good influences. At the worst, they affect only the bark and do not injure the system like the rust of inaction.

Dr. Samuel Gridley Howe

The Blind Child in the Regular Kindergarten

by

Josephine Stratton

Teacher
Norwich Central Schools
Norwich, New York

Charles C Thomas • Publisher
Springfield • Illinois • U.S.A.

Published and Distributed Throughout the World by

CHARLES C THOMAS • PUBLISHER

Bannerstone House

301-327 East Lawrence Avenue, Springfield, Illinois, U.S.A.

1977, by CHARLES C THOMAS • PUBLISHER

ISBN 0-398-03623-3

Library of Congress Catalog Card Number: 76-44517

*With THOMAS BOOKS careful attention is given to all details of
manufacturing and design. It is the Publisher's desire to present books that are
satisfactory as to their physical qualities and artistic possibilities and
appropriate for their particular use. THOMAS BOOKS will be true to those
laws of quality that assure a good name and good will.*

Printed in the United States of America

R-2

Library of Congress Cataloging in Publication Data

Stratton, Josephine.
    The blind child in the regular kindergarten.

    Bibliography: p.
    Includes index.
    1. Blind—Education. 2. Kindergarten. I. Title.
HV1643.S8   372.21'8   76-44517

to
LISA

---

who, though blind,
sees the world with the same wonderment
and delight as
children the world over . . . . .

Acknowledgments

I wish to express my appreciation to the people who helped make this book possible. First, I want to thank the staff members at Perry Browne School, Norwich, New York: Charlotte Aldrich, Principal, for her continued support and guidance in our efforts; Karen Wright, kindergarten teacher, and Jeanne Crawford, first grade teacher, for their sensitive understanding and their ingenuity in dealing with the day-to-day problems encountered in having a blind child in their regular classrooms; Doris Mason, teacher's aide, for her dedication in providing the necessary individual help; Peg Ingersoll, physical education teacher, for her insight and knowledge in developing body image and motor skills; Dawne Berberich, Peg Bennett, Kate Stewart, and Joyce Lawson, kindergarten and first grade teachers, for helping to organize and analyze activities; and all the staff members who helped in any way to make the mainstreaming a positive and successful experience.

In addition, I want to thank Mr. William Berinati, Orientation and Mobility Specialist, Blind Work Association, Binghamton, New York, for helping in our efforts to devise ways to train mobility skills; Jane Deniston, Blind Work Association, Binghamton, New York, and LaVerne Tupper, New York State Commission for the Blind, for their suggestions in specific areas concerning the blind; Doris S. Lake, State University College, Oneonta, New York, for her encouragement and assistance in organizing and preparing the material; Cheryl Curnalia, typist, for patiently typing and retyping the manuscript.

THE RIGHT

to remain at home with his own family and in his own community while he receives his education

to enjoy the same broad and fulfilling experiences in school as every other child does, limited only by his blindness

to an education that demands the development of his full potential

to be accepted and loved, first as a child with his own pattern of strengths and weaknesses, his own learning style and personality, but with the added inconvenience of being blind

to be disciplined as other children are in a way that will help him learn to grow into a responsible person

to be free from overprotection that will stifle growth and interfere with his development of independence

to move around freely and independently as much as possible to explore and learn from his environment even if this may sometimes result in small mishaps

to be treated inconspicuously in the group, gradually learning to make most of the adjustments to the sighted world himself, as that is the way it will be all of his life

to learn the special skills he needs because of his blindness, and to have access to the necessary special training and equipment

to develop satisfying friendships that provide him with love, security, and happiness

BILL OF RIGHTS FOR THE BLIND

---

in the regular classroom

Introduction

With the rapidly increasing practice of mainstreaming many handicapped children, the critical lack of both information and materials for the classroom teacher to use with a blind child becomes immediately apparent. While the help of a specialist is not necessarily required to educate the blind child in the regular kindergarten, the need for more guidelines than are now available is definitely urgent.

The purpose of this book is two-fold: first, to review the literature on the learning behaviors of the blind child to determine if the techniques and materials used to develop his reading readiness should be the same as or different from those used for the sighted child; second, to provide for the kindergarten teacher a guide which has a rationale for selecting activities for the blind child that is based on sound principles of child development. In this guide, activities commonly used in kindergarten curriculums are listed and coded to show which ones need no adapting for the blind child, which require some adapting and which activities are totally inappropriate.

The philosophy underlying this book is that the blind child is first of all a child, more clearly resembling all other children than differing from them, and that the similarity of his "childness" must never be allowed to be obscured by the difference of his blindness. He is not a "blind child," but a child — like any other child — who just happens to be blind. Differences among blind children are as varying as differences among all children. Therefore, we must approach the blind learner first as a child, as an individual with his own pattern of strengths and weaknesses, with his own learning style and personality, but with the limitations of lack of vision.

The concept of education for handicapped children is changing abruptly. The previously accepted practice of classifying, thus labeling, handicapped children for segregation into special classes for "special" educational programs is being reexamined, restructured, and sometimes abolished completely. The legality of special classes is being debated in courts across the country, the educational benefits to the child are being questioned by parents and educators alike, and the effects of special class placement on the self image of the child are being seriously pondered by all. Adding impetus to this change in thinking, and in an attempt to avoid discrimination, legislators are passing laws mandating the right of handicapped children to an education that meets their speical needs right in the regular classroom. New York State has increased the state aid to schools (up to double, depending on the handicap) for any handicapped child educated in the local public schools.

This author, faced with the reality and the challenge of assisting in a day-to-day education of a blind child in kindergarten, was appalled at the state of education for the young blind child. Much time was wasted trying to locate materials that, when finally found, proved often to be out of date, inappropriate, or uninteresting for young children, and definitely not based on sound principles of child development. Inquiries sometimes resulted in help, but more often just discouragingly pointed up the confusion and barrenness of the field. In rural areas, especially, where the incidence of blind children in public schools is small, educational services for the blind are extremely limited, scattered, and irregular. Even the possibility of talking to another teacher who has had experience with a blind child may be nonexistent. Neither are courses for teachers readily available. For instance, a survey in New York State, including an inquiry to the State Education Department, showed that only two centers in that state offer courses on teaching the blind: Dominican College in Blauvelt (undergraduate only) and Teachers' College, Columbia University. A listing from the American Foundation for the Blind shows a similar situation in the other states.

Research and literature on educating the young blind child, in contrast to educating children with other handicaps, was found to be sparse, difficult to locate, and dated by some fifteen, twenty, or more years. Much of this research was done with adults, often ones in residential institutions, and with blinded veterans of World War II, by investigators interested primarily in the blindness itself. The knowledge gained was then applied to the education of children with little regard for the difference between the learning of adults and that of children. Encouragingly, in the last few years, some research has been done specifically on educating young blind children even in settings other than institutions. However, this research, while enlightening in itself, has not been translated into programs for use by the teacher in the public school.

This author believes that the approach to and the focus of the education of the blind child must be reversed; it must start with the child, not with his blindness; and the materials, methods, and programs developed must be based on known principles of child development. Historically, there seems to be little evidence that this has been the case. The author further believes that the regular classroom teacher is the one who can most effectively reverse the approach to the education of blind children from one that is "blind-oriented" to one that is "child-oriented." Although not a specialist in blindness, the primary teacher by training and by commitment, is a specialist in children. The classroom teacher's strong background in child development and the expertise in planning and implementing programs in a classroom situation can both be important factors in influencing the approach to educating the blind child. The classroom teacher in the public school faces daily a wide diversity of levels and patterns in the development of children. This serves to keep the teacher constantly aware, not only of the differences and uniqueness of each child, but, more importantly, the commonalities that all children share in the process of growing and developing. The blind child is no different. The emphasis of his educational program must be, not on the differences due to his blindness, but on the commonalities that he shares with all children, with provisions made for variations due to his own individuality and to the limitations of his blindness.

This author believes that the blind child gains many benefits from being educated in the local public school with sighted children. Further, many of these benefits are inherent in the situation itself and, therefore, cannot be gained in a school for the blind. The child will feel like everyone else when he can go to school right along with his neighbors and friends. He will gain in confidence when he realizes that he can do many of the same things that his friends do. He will learn to feel comfortable with sighted people in the sighted world where he will live and work all his life. He will be more stimulated and will broaden his experiences more by interacting with sighted children than with only the blind. In a heterogeneous class in the public school, his "childness" and "normalcy" will be more readily perceived and focused on; in a class of all blind children, his blindness too often and too easily becomes the dominant focus.

The challenge to teachers in the regular classroom is clear: the challenge of providing an education for the blind child, as for the sighted, that allows him to develop, to grow, and to learn with his friends as all children do; the challenge of adjusting the regular curriculum, when necessary, to allow him to learn in the ways that he can; and the challenge of helping him learn the special skills that he needs because of his blindness.

Contents

Acknowledgments vii
Introduction xi

1. Early Development of the Blind Child 3
2. Implications for Education 15
3. Special Concerns in Educating the Blind Child 17
4. Evaluation of the Blind Child in Kindergarten 25

A. Kindergarten Activities Coded for Use
   with a Blind Child 31
B. Adjusted Activities for the Blind Child 45
C. Recipes for Tactile Materials 59
D. Equipment for the Blind Child in Kindergarten 61
E. Sources of Help and Information 63
F. Suggested Readings for Teachers 69
G. Definitions 75

Bibliography 81
Index 85

The Blind Child in the Regular Kindergarten

Chapter 1

Early Development of the Blind Child

Early Years

IT HAS been said that the ideal time for a person to lose his sight is between the ages of ten and twenty-five. At this point, he will have had the benefits of vision in his earliest years of learning, yet is still young enough to make the necessary adjustments. [12]

The choice of time is not ours to make, but the age at which the child goes blind will have a significant impact on his later learning. The congenitally blind child, blind from birth, never has vision to facilitate even his most basic development, such as playing with his hands, but must coordinate all of his development and learning through his remaining senses. On the other hand the adventitiously blind child, even though he will also need to coordinate through his other senses, has the added advantage of visual memory, since

3

he has had at least partial vision during some part of his life. He knows what a house looks like, what a tree looks like, what the members of his family look like. The effectiveness of his visual memory will depend to a great extent on the age at which he became blind. Any amount of vision in his early years greatly facilitates and changes his later learning.[24]

In his first few weeks of life, the blind child has an even greater need for stimulation than does the sighted child, as he is extremely passive and quiet. He needs to be held, to be played with, and to be part of family activities when awake. But it is at this same point that the parents are usually struggling with their own feelings of acceptance toward their blind child. Their initial reaction of shock may be followed by rejection, depression, general inability to face the problem. They may become so involved with the blindness that they become ineffective in meeting the child's immediate basic needs. So at the very time when the blind child needs even more stimulation than the sighted child, he in fact probably gets less. It takes time for parents to work through their own feelings. Counseling at this time can be most beneficial. Parents can learn to understand and provide for the normal and special needs of their blind child, and eventually accept the child himself as well as the blindness.[18]

The classroom teacher's initial reaction to having a blind child in class for the first time may follow a similar pattern in a less extreme way. Understanding and remaining alert to the possible reactions and adjustment period she herself may undergo should help to prevent focusing first and exclusively on the blindness which in this case happens to be in the form of a child, and enable her to focus on the child himself with his own individuality who just happens to be blind.

The conclusions of a University of Chicago study[25] done with blind children again emphasizes the importance of the effect of the family and the environment on the blind child's development and functioning. It concludes that "deficits usually attributed to blindness are related primarily not to the physical handicap in and of itself but to limitations in the 'opportunities for learning' which are experienced by the child." It also states that the blind child is a vulnerable child and suffers to an extreme degree from any condition unfavorable to growth and development.

Moor[1] also stresses the importance of the attitudes of the family and the home environment in the growth of the preschool blind child. The child needs the feeling of belonging, concrete evidence of the parents' love, the opportunity to explore and learn through experience, to come to know his own ability and worth, and to develop independence. The blind child has the same feelings and interest in his environment as the sighted child, but he must depend more upon his opportunities to explore and upon other people to bring the world to him. These people are first his family and later, his friends and the school. The significance of the quality of the early family relationships as they affect the development of the young blind child must therefore be reemphasized.

Motor Development

The blind child will, generally speaking, go through the same steps in developing gross motor skills as the sighted child, but at certain stages both the method of learning and the pace of learning will vary from that of the sighted child. Without vision, he will need to depend on auditory clues and on ear-hand coordination to coordinate his gross motor movements. These are less exact and harder to perceive than the visual. This may not significantly affect motor development during the first few months. However, he will probably not learn to creep until ear-hand coordination develops at about the end of the first year.[9] Even then, he will need a great deal of incentive and encouragement to move about. He should be encouraged to move toward familiar sounds, as the sound of his mother's voice, or toward a "reward" that he likes such as a favorite toy or a cookie.

Lacking the visual models, the blind child is unable to imitate others in even such everyday activities as sitting, creeping, standing, or walking. If left on his own, he would probably devise ways to move around, but these ways may lack efficiency and safety.[22] He needs guidance right from the start to learn locomotor skills that are efficient, safe, and socially acceptable, and ones that will not need to be unlearned later. He may initially need to be placed in the appropriate position and have his arms and legs moved for him. In learning to walk, he may benefit from having his feet placed on top of his parent's feet while the parent walks in normal steps. Later, he may need similar help in learning to jump, do animal walks, climb, etc. Familiarity and certainty in his environment will encourage free and natural movements, leading to good muscular growth and good health; uncertainty will cause inhibited movements resulting in posture abnormalities, poor gait, and inefficient body movements.

Optimum motor development is as important for the blind as for the sighted. Body movement forms the base for good muscular development and for correct posture and gait. It forms the base for the development of body image, laterality and directionality, tactile discrimination, and for concepts of space. For the blind child, all aspects of movements in the early years form the foundation on which orientation and mobility skills will later be built. The classroom teacher, because of daily contact with the young blind child, has an important responsibility to guide, encourage, and directly teach the appropriate motor skills.

Tactile Development

It is often assumed that when one loses the use of one sense, the others automatically compensate by becoming keener. This would certainly facilitate the learning for the blind child, but, unfortunately, this is not the case. Unless he develops his remaining senses through persistent training, he will get little more information from them than does the sighted child.

The tactile sense is one of the two most important avenues through which a blind child gets information and meaning from his environment. (The other avenue is auditory-language.) The development of tactile skills in the blind child follows the same general progression as in the sighted child. However, there are two important differences, one in the method of learning and the other in the final goal: First, the blind child needs much more stimulation and motivation over a longer period of time to achieve the same tactile learning as the sighted child; second, he must develop his tactile skills to a much higher degree than the sighted child.

Stimulation to develop the tactile sense must begin in the early weeks of life. The blind infant needs to have toys within arm's reach in the crib so he will touch them as he moves. He needs to be encouraged to reach toward the sound of a rattle in the same way a sighted child reaches when he sees one. He needs many opportunities to explore freely as he begins to move around. According to one research study done by the American Foundation for the Blind, the blind child who has been free to explore in his earliest years subsequently developed much better ability in using his hands than the one who had been overprotected with limited experiences. [1] The blind child may have been limited in his free exploring because the adults around him were fearful and unduly concerned for his safety. He may have had limited exploring because it was easier for him to function within known and familiar limits than to step out into the unknown. He will probably need to be encouraged persistently to explore because he lacks the visual stimulus that makes the sighted child curious.

Conclusive research on the specific development of tactile skills in the blind is limited. However, there are some research findings on tactile development that are pertinent to the education of the young blind child. One study done by Nolan showed that tactile ability increased with age, suggesting that maturity is an influencing factor.[26] Another study by Weiner [26] suggests that tactile skills can be improved through training; Kephart [15] and Frostig [6], in their work on visual perception, support the belief that perceptual skills can be trained.

Hampshire states that the congenitally blind child has to be taught to use his tactile sense in the same way that a sighted child is taught to use his vision.[11] He considers the tactile sense a "dynamic" sense, adapting to the functional demands on it. He states further that, if given optimum chance to develop, the tactile sense could very significantly increase the capabilities of blind people.

Rogow [28], in a study on perceptual organization in the blind, states: "Research data on blindness suggests that visual impairment does not prevent or even delay the development of efficient information processing." She found that the response level of young blind children on tactile perception tasks matched the developmental stages outlined by Piaget for all children.

The tactile sense is of vital importance to the education of the blind child. The goal in guiding its development is to lead the child gradually from gross discrimination of objects in his environment to fine discrimination involving small muscles and finger tips. The developmental progression is the same as for a sighted child, but the importance to the child who is blind is greater. The use of the tactile sense can make a significant contribution to the blind child's growth and learning only if he learns to use it in a discriminating, systematic, and efficient manner. The importance of early training and guidance in this area both at home and at school cannot be overemphasized, as the tactile sense will be one of the major sources of interaction and learning for the blind child all his life.

Auditory and Language Development

The auditory-language system parallels the tactile in importance for the blind child as an avenue for getting information and meaning from his environment. As stated previously, other senses do not automatically compensate when the use of another sense is lost. Nevertheless, many blind people do seem to have better-than-average auditory skills. This is due, not to innate superior ability of this sense, but to its exceptional development through training and the demand for its use. The development of auditory and language skills is extremely important for the blind child as he extends his real world beyond the reach and touch of his arms and hands.

The blind child's auditory development may be slow for the first two years. Lairy and Harrison-Corvello found that even the orientation to noise developed later, about the seventh month as compared to second month for the sighted. [18] Rogow concluded that during the latter half of the first year, the blind infant learns to use sound, independent of tactual perception, to perceive the presence of an object. [28] Further, he later learns to judge distance by variations and localization of sounds; and he perceives relationships of objects, not as whole objects, but as a series of sequential auditory perceptions.

Stimulation of the auditory sense must begin in the earliest weeks of the blind infant's life. He needs to be talked to even more than the sighted child, the warmth of the familiar voice far more important than what is said. He needs the contact of a familiar voice to be reassured of the nearness of his family. The family that is not naturally very talkative must make a very conscious effort to talk to the blind infant. Sounds tend to come and go out of nothingness for the blind, so the recurring sound of the familiar voice will help him learn that sounds do in fact have an origin and meaning. The use of the radio, television, or records, important as they are for stimulating learning and adding new dimensions, can never be a substitute for the warmth of human contact. The excessive use of these to entertain the blind child, and the important words here are "excessive" and "entertain," can actually impede his progress in many areas; what he needs from his family at this time is active participation and stimulation.

The blind child must learn an ever-increasing discrimination of sounds in his environment. He must learn through sound, as well as touch, when to be careful, afraid, or happy, when to respond with love, with a question, or with action. He will learn to discern what direction a sound comes from, to identify who is coming from the sound of the footsteps, to know he is near the cafeteria when he hears the sound of dishes. As he grows older he will learn to cross streets safely by listening for the direction and flow of traffic.

Growing out of the early development of auditory skills is the development of language. This is even more vital for the blind child than for the sighted. Without vision, more of his learning and communication is dependent upon his understanding and use of language. As soon as the young child begins to understand words, it is important that he hears language that is meaningful to him. His experience and activities should be verbalized. For instance, when the child is washing his hands, the actions might be explained: "The water is running. I am washing your fingers. You are splashing the water." It is so important that parents make an effort to communicate through words, as the child cannot respond to facial expressions, eye contact, or other actions. Without words, he is to a great extent cut off from the world.

Language development progresses from the naming of concrete things and actions, to the language used to describe feelings and attitudes, and finally to the use of language for abstract ideas.[9] Language growth and comprehension are directly related to the growth and development of concepts. The blind child must have a solid base of concrete experience before he can understand the language that describes them.

He needs many experiences with objects that are alike and different, long and short, smooth and rough, before he can understand these abstract concepts and the language that describes them. This author agrees that the sequence of language development must first start from concrete experience, and that the child must next relate his emerging language skills to his known tactile and concrete experiences. But this author further believes that the child must develop his language to the point that he can reverse the process and gain new "experience" and understandings solely through the use of language, i.e. gain the ability to use language as the primary referent for receiving new concepts and learnings. This would not decrease the importance of basing language on concrete sensory experiences, but would extend the language horizons for the blind beyond that which is able to be experienced directly through the senses.

One reason for so much concern in the literature about relating language to the concrete experience is to prevent "verbalisms," a much talked about phenomenon in the education of the blind. Verbalisms are defined as the blind person's use of words whose meanings can be understood only through vision, such as green, foggy, dark. The implication is that the blind person can have no understanding of such terms as understanding must depend upon the sense of vision. Dobecki reviewed the research on this point and questioned the assumption that verbalisms are necessarily meaningless to the blind just because they are based on visual impressions.[4] He proposes that to use an approach to language that is based solely on experience through the sense is to ignore the important relationship of words to words. He maintains that, while meaningless verbalisms in the blind may be detrimental to the development of language, the overconcern that has been generated for verbalisms can itself be a delimiting factor. Sensory experiences are not the only factors forming the base on which language may be built, and language need not be limited to this. In addition, it may be built within a framework of emotional, situational, or contextual meaning.

Teachers in the primary classroom are in an ideal situation for helping the blind child build meaningful auditory and language skills. Field trips (even around the school yard), extensive use of ordinary manipulative materials, social play involving conversation about the activities, finger plays, and the many stories used in the primary grades are all excellent ways to stimulate language development, excellent for the blind as well as for the sighted.

Social Development

The social development of the blind preschool child, as with the sighted, will vary according to the extent of his opportunities to meet and interact with others. He needs many experiences during his early years to make friends outside the family primarily for the enjoyment that this will bring him, but also for the needed stimulation and broadening of his world. It will take real effort on the part of the parents and teachers to initiate active social experiences, rather than to allow the blind child's natural passiveness to keep him on the fringes of or apart from surrounding social groups.

The blind child will need extra help to make contact with his peers because he cannot see how others play or even that they are near. Children with whom he is in frequent contact will soon learn by observation and experience that the blind child needs objects put into his hand instead of just handed to him silently, needs spoken directions rather than motions, and responds more happily to the guidance of a voice than to being led or pushed around. The blind child will benefit from planned and structured social experiences, at least at first. In this way he can learn the easy give and take of playing with others in steps that are appropriate and comfortable for him. Then these experiences will be happy ones for him right from the start.

The ease of adjustment for any child entering nursery school or kindergarten depends to a great extent upon his adjustment to others. For most children, at this time, it requires a refining of their ability to adjust their needs to the needs of the group. This is basically no different for the blind child. His adjustment to working as a member of a larger group will be more comfortable if he has had many experiences playing with other children. However, due to his lack of vision, he may appear to show little respect for the rights of others in the group, as he is hampered in his ability to realize exactly what a group is and how many other children also need to share the teacher's time and attention. This usually does not reflect a behavior problem, but a lack of understanding of the situation caused and complicated by the lack of vision. For example, if he could see the long line of children waiting for a turn on the slide, he could more quickly grasp the need for sharing in the group. Because he is unable to maintain a visual contact with the teacher, as sighted children do constantly, he will need to hear her voice often or to receive an occasional touch to reassure him that the teacher is near.

Parents and teachers need to keep in mind that the goal for the blind child's social development is to help him to actively grow toward social relations that are satisfying and responsible, and to avoid letting him become the victim of come-as-it-may approach which often results in passive, dependent, and overprotecting contacts with others.

Self-Care Skills

A blind child can learn many self-care skills almost as early as the sighted child if ways of teaching are used which are compatible with both his abilities and his limitations. [23] Toilet training and dressing are two examples of this. The feeding of oneself, which the sighted child learns through imitation, is a much slower learning process for the blind child. Groves and Griffith [7] suggest letting the child finger feed himself (even food not usually considered finger food) until around the age of four when a real attempt should be made to help him learn to use a spoon. Using the knife for spreading may be learned from the ages of eight to ten; cutting should not be attempted until age twelve. Definite suggestions for teaching eating skills are given in this pamphlet. However, Maxfield and Bucholz include these skills at a somewhat earlier age on their Social Maturity Scale. [22]

SUMMARY

The blind child can be expected to do most of the same things that the sighted child does, some at the same age and others at a later age. The way that this is accomplished may or may not be the same as for sighted children. Generally, he will need more active intervention from others to achieve the expected, complete level of development. Given optimum intervention, his ultimate level of development will be similar to that of the sighted in most cases.

He will need direct teaching of some skills that the sighted child learns quite naturally through imitation. Kurzhals states that a blind child will never be "ready" without a great deal of extra stimulation and direct teaching, and every action must be taught slowly and patiently. [17] He does not learn instinctively — he must be taught.

To guide a blind child in his development we must know what to expect of all children at various ages and then adapt for the blind child. Otherwise, we run the risk of becoming so involved with the blindness that we do not see the normal patterns as they develop. [23] The child, as a child, must always have first consideration; his blindness falls into reasonable perspective after that.

Chapter 2

Implications for Education

1. The blind child may need to be taught directly some seemingly easy skills that the sighted child learns almost spontaneously through imitation.

2. The blind child was not born with superior auditory or tactile skills; he does need extra training in these to insure their maximum functioning as his two most important avenues for learning.

3. The blind child must learn without the aid of visual imitation, often requiring him to skip over several intervening steps involving vision to the harder step not involving vision. Tying shoes is an example of this.

4. Many problems that arise will most likely be due to causes not related to the blindness and that also occur in sighted children — sharing, separating from home, adjusting to group living.

5. If the blind child shows retarded development in some areas it may be due to insufficient stimulation and

opportunity to learn rather than to the physical disability or to an actual inability to learn. He probably is "untaught" rather than "unteachable."

6. It is not the visual impairment that itself is of primary importance, but how competently the child learns to live with his impairment without allowing it to become unnecessarily handicapping.

7. The blind child may have a tendency to develop verbal skills based on imitation rather than on meaning. Care must be exercised to insure that the developing language skills are meaningful to the child.

8. There are some areas in which the blind child must fail. He needs guidance to accept this and to learn to accept help graciously in these areas.

9. A blind child may have difficulty forming concepts as he must manipulate from the parts to the whole. He may form some inaccurate conclusions as did the blind men in the story, *The Blind Men and the Elephant.*© [29]

10. Problems that the blind child encounters in learning must never be allowed to become barriers.

11. "Blindness is a physical nuisance, an inconvenience which makes it necessary to learn other ways of doing what most people do with the aid of sight. The important fact is that these ways do exist, and that they work . . ." [1]

Chapter 3

Special Concerns in Educating the Blind Child

Blindisms

BLINDISMS are mannerisms that are quite characteristic of the blind, such as eye poking, rocking, shaking hands in a tense way, and head shaking. Most blind children go through stages of these mannerisms in their normal pattern of growth. Authorities generally agree that blindisms are the result of understimulation. In the primary-age school child these blindisms themselves are not a cause for concern, but any inefficient performance caused by them, as in reading or mobility, must be called to his attention. He should not be scolded for his mannerisms, but gentle reminding may be effective and appropriate for some children. For social reasons it is well to help the blind child drop his mannerisms as soon as it is comfortable for him to do so. This may be

17

compared to thumb sucking. It is socially acceptable in most groups for a very young child to suck his thumb, but an older child is usually ridiculed for it. The most effective way to help a child overcome his mannerisms is to provide him with many materials and activities of real interest to him. Even then, direct encouragement to participate may be necessary.

OVERPROTECTION

One of the blind child's greatest needs is to be self-reliant and independent, learning to do things for himself appropriate to his age. Over-protection is not a kindness to him, but is a needless disservice that seriously adds to his problems. Overprotection implies that we do not realistically accept the blind child as a person in his own right, capable of functioning on his own. In the long haul, it undermines his security making him fear the consequences of the loss of this protection. If he has developed independence, however, he no longer needs to fear changes or unexplored situations as he can rely on his own resources. Overprotection can be stifling to the child, affecting the development of his personality, social relations, achievement, and safety.

The kindest thing that we can do for the blind child, and probably the hardest, is to avoid overprotection at all costs. Teach him how to and then insist that he function independently. The manner and example of the classroom teacher will go far in setting the course for preventing or eliminating overprotection by peers as well as by well-meaning adults at school. Frequent communcations with the family will help promote uniformity of expectations at home and at school.

LATERALITY AND DIRECTIONALITY

Laterality is the internal awareness of the two sides of the body, involving the ability to distinguish the separateness of these two sides. Laterality is the foundation on which directionality is established. Directionality is the projection of the internal laterality outward to objects in space.

Well-developed laterality is crucial for the blind child. It forms the basis for learning the real relationships of the parts of his own body, attaining good posture, establishing the location of objects, and moving around safely and confidently in his environment. It forms a stable reference point for understanding space and the relation of objects in space. It forms the base for learning to distinguish letters without confusing ones that have an exact reversal pattern in Braille. (This is no small consideration, as there are seventeen pairs of direct lateral reversals in the formations of Braille letters and common contractions used even in the preprimer reading. There are also many exact vertical inversions. And to think we worry about sighted children reversing b and d, m and w, was and saw!)

Laterality needs to be distinguished from the naming of the right and left. A child may be able to name his right and left hand correctly and still not have an adequate inner development of laterality. He may know which is his right hand because it happens to have a scar on it, or his left hand is the one he colors with. Ability to identify right and left by name is not a test of his laterality and may have no relation to his inner awareness of sidedness.[15]

Laterality is a learned skill. It can be learned through motor activities that involve bilateral, unilateral, and alternating lateral movements. Bilateral activities require the use of both sides of the body in the same way at the same time, such as jumping jacks or rabbit hops. Unilateral activities involve the use of one side of the body independently, such as hopping on one foot or ball play with one hand. Alternating lateral activities require that the two sides are used alternately to complement each other, as in running, climbing, balancing, and cutting. By experimenting and gaining control of his body in activities such as these, he will gain the inner sense of the separateness of the sides of his body.

When laterality is becoming firmly established, the child can begin to relate objects in space to his own known sidedness. He is thereby transferring his laterality to directionality. Without vision, the blind child must rely on auditory and tactile cues to determine directions. To a far greater extent than his sighted peers, he must depend on directionality and on his full awareness of right and left, up and down, forward, backward, and sideways to move freely in his environment.

Many activities normally done in the primary classroom and physical education classes will enhance the development of laterality and directionality in the blind child as well as in the sighted. The teacher must remain alert to the importance of insuring that the child's laterality is based solidly on an inner awareness and is not merely the ability to name right and left. This is especially important for the blind child as a readiness for later orientation and mobility training.

ORIENTATION AND MOBILITY

Orientation is one's use of his remaining senses to establish his position and relationship to other objects in the environment.

Mobility is one's actual locomotion from a starting point to a desired location in another part of the environment.[21]

Orientation and mobility training is the door to freedom for the blind. Instruction in these areas is an on-going, never-ending process and must be a cooperative effort shared by many. The formal aspect of this training is done by a qualified mobility specialist.*

It is estimated that from 250 to 300 hours are needed for a specialist to train a congenitally blind person in full orientation and mobility.[21] The majority of this time is taken up in

---

*For information on having the free service of a mobility specialist help a blind child in your school, contact your State Department for Handicapped Children.

orientation, which has its base in the development of the other senses from infancy on. Sensory awareness—sounds, smells, textures, temperatures — can give valuable clues in identifying locations in space. Body image, laterality, directionality, motor coordination, manipulation are all important skills that contribute to the development of space concepts that underly orientation and mobility. The mobility specialist will be hampered in trying to train the blind child who has not adequately developed these basic concepts of self and space. The importance of this training was pointed up recently.[16] A nineteen-year-old man, even though he had attended a state school for the blind for fourteen years, had been partially confined to his home because of inability to find his way around, needing a sighted guide to take him to his work at the workshop. With the training from a mobility speacialist he is learning to get around by himself, even crossing busy intersections. This represents real freedom for a blind person.

Teaching of these skills, as with all teaching, is most effective if begun at appropriate developmental stages of the child and reinforced over a period of time suited to the individual. Piaget notes that if concepts have not been introduced and learned at the maturational stage at which they are ready to be learned, they are lost.[21] Also, Lydon and McGraw[21] state:

> There is strong evidence that basic concepts, such as those relevant to body image and spatial organization, must be introduced and learned at the maturational stage at which they are ready to be learned, or they are lost or exceedingly difficult to learn. The sighted child gradually learns these concepts, through vision, from infancy. The child who is congenitally blind does not and so seriously lags in concept development through adolescence. One of the learning areas that this deficiency most affects is orientation and mobility.

These authors recommend the incorporation of concept development into the total program from kindergarten on.

Classroom teachers have a vital role in providing opportunities for these skills to develop in the early years and to teach them directly if they do not develop. It is important also, since the classroom teacher spends a longer time with the child daily, that he can initiate the teaching at the appropriate maturational time for the child and will be able to space the practice and reinforcement to meet his needs. The role of the classroom teacher in orientation and mobility is a primary, not a secondary, one even though in no way will he do the formal training. It is primary because the training the teacher gives forms the foundation for the later formal training. It is primary because it contributes in a very direct way to the blind child's ease and success in becoming independent.

ORGANIZATIONAL SKILLS

Many young children are unorganized, if not actually disorganized. Organization is not a natural characteristic of the young child. It is learned either from imitation and practice in an organized home, or it is gradually learned in the first few years of school as the condition of group living and the necessity to accomplish work promote it. There are some who place little value on organizational skills for the young child, placing many other things ahead in importance. Be that as it may, organizational skills for the blind child can never be simply a matter of preference, differing values, or a chosen life style. An organized approach will be the only way he will be able to accomplish some tasks independently or even at all. An organized approach will go a long way toward lessening frustrations and increasing his satisfaction in a task. Keeping his clothes in a certain arrangement in the drawer will enable him to dress himself without confusion or frustration. Arranging his food and table service in a certain way each time will enable him to eat with little or no help. Gaining the habit of putting away his things where they belong and remembering where he put them will make him independent in keeping track of his belongings. Arranging his own work materials at school in a definite place and order (using a tray for this is invaluable) will help him to accomplish learning tasks with less frustration and consequently more learning.

The classroom teacher will need to be more precise for the blind child than for the sighted in working toward effective organization. Well-established organization is not the goal itself, but a very important way, in some instances the only way, to the goal of increased independent functioning for the blind child.

Chapter 4

Evaluation of the Blind Child in Kindergarten

T HE SOCIAL Maturity Scale for Blind Preschool Children is based on Edgar Doll's
Vineland Social Maturity Scale.[22] It is an
interview type test, and the person supplying the information
concerning the blind child should know the child intimately.
The test should be administered by an examiner who has had
much experience with the psychological testing of small
children and also with diagnostic interviewing of both
children and adults. This is not an intelligence test, but an
assessment of the child's level of social competence, yielding
a Social Quotient based on the performance of other blind
children in the same age range. It contains ninety-five items,
each placed within the age level of expected performance
from birth to six years. The manual contains, in addition to
the scale itself, a thorough explanation of procedures for
administering, directions for scoring, and examples of acceptable behaviors for each item. The cost is 75 cents for the
manual and one test form; additional test forms are 8 cents.

BODY-IMAGE OF BLIND CHILDREN

Bryant Cratty has done extensive work on the development of body-image and body movement, with all children and has developed a survey type test that can be easily administered by the classroom teacher. It assesses the level that the child has already reached in each of certain specific behaviors relating to body-image. Some age-level data is given for the responses, but no "score" is assigned to the child's performance. The areas tested include identification of body parts, body movement, laterality, and directionality in self and others. It evaluates the child's ability to make left-right judgements about his body and to judge the location of objects in relation to his own body.

Cratty points out that one limitation of the test is that it is directly dependent on the child's ability to respond to verbal directions. He mentions that a mannikin construction survey has been suggested for younger children.[3] The cost is $1.50 for the manual which includes a test form.

ROUGHNESS DISCRIMINATION TEST

Available from the American Printing House for the Blind, 1839 Frankfort Avenue, Louisville, Kentucky 40206, the Roughness Discrimination Test was developed to predict readiness to learn to read Braille for blind children in first grade. The test consists of a set of sixty-nine cards on which are mounted four pieces of sandpaper. Of these, three are alike and one is different, being rougher or coarser than the other three. The child must find the sandpaper that is different. The standardization was found to have substantial predictive validity and high reliability. The entire test kit consists of the set of cards, a manual, and twenty-five self-scoring answer sheets. The cost of the entire kit is $32.00.

PSYCHOLOGICAL TESTING

An examiner experienced in administering psychological tests to young children can get a fair estimate of the blind child's intellectual functioning level by adapting the commonly used intelligence scales.

Appendices

Appendix A

Kindergarten Activities

Coded for use with a Blind Child

MANY activities used in the regular kindergarten will be as appropriate for the blind child as for the sighted child. However, some will need to be adjusted, and some will be totally inappropriate. The activities listed on the following pages are coded to aid the classroom teacher in selection, adjusting, or providing alternative learning activities when necessary.

Code:

- No mark in the Code column means that the activity needs no adjusting for the blind child.

- An asterisk in the Code column means that the activity needs no adjusting, but the mode of learning or the outcomes of the learning will be different for the blind child. For instance, painting may be done by the blind child, but it becomes only a kinesthetic activity instead of the kinesthetic-visual activity it is for the sighted.

- A letter and numbers in the Code column means that the activity needs adjusting for the blind child. Suggestions for adjusting are in the "Adjusted Activities" section immediately following this activity section. The adjusted activity is coded with the same letter and numbers as appear in the Code column. For instance, if II A 5 appears in the Code column, the adjustment for the activity will be found in the "Adjusted Activities" section under II A 5.

- A black box in the Code column means that the activity is not appropriate for the blind child.

Modality:

- **K** means that the activity involves the kinesthestic (movement) sense.

- **T** means that the activity involves the tactile sense.

- **A** means that the activity involves the auditory sense.

- **V** means that the activity involves the visual sense.

ACTIVITIES

I. BODY IMAGE

Skill	Activity	Modality	Procedure	Code
A. Identifying body parts.	1. Name body parts	K A	Teacher names part; child touches it.	
	2. Hokey-Pokey	K A	Usual procedure.	
	3. Trace around own body form	K T V	Trace around each other's body; color, cut out; hang up for comparison with self.	I A 3
			Trace around hands and feet; cut and compare.	I A 3
	4. Construct body form	T	Make a person with play dough.	
	5. Puzzles	T V	Put together large puzzles of people.	
	6. Make puzzle	T V	Make own puzzles using own picture or pictures of people.	I A 6
	7. Assemble a person	T V	Use precut paper shapes to form a person's body.	I A 7
	8. Missing parts	V	Identify the parts missing on a drawing of a person.	

II. GROSS MOTOR COORDINATION

Skill	Activity	Modality	Procedure	Code
A. Body Movement	1. Climbing	K	Playground equipment.	
	2. Rhythms	K A	Routine classroom procedures.	
	3. Bag jump	K	Put both feet in burlap bag; jump.	
	4. Crawl box	K	Cut a box so child can lie across it with head, arms, legs sticking out like a turtle. Crawl, using both arms pulling feet along; use one arm only; use alternating arms.	
	5. Animal walks	K	Rabbit hops, seal walk, duck walk, etc.	II A 5
	6. Running	K		II A 6
	7. Jumping jacks	K		II A 7
	8. Simon Says	K V	Usual procedure.	II A 8
	9. Freeze tag or Statues	K A	Children move about freely, perhaps to music; when leader gives signal, children must stop and hold that position.	

Skill	Activity	Modality	Procedure	Code
B. Laterality	1. Walking beam	K V	Walk across a board (2" x 4") that is suspended a few inches or more from the floor. Look at visual target while walking.	II B 1
	2. Angels-in-the-snow	K V K A K T	Lie on floor. On command (visual, auditory, tactile) child moves; first, both arms up over head to touch at top; then, both legs out; arms and legs at same time; left arm and left leg; right arm and right leg, etc.	II B 2
	3. Trampoline	K	Do individually with Physical Education teacher.	
	4. Leg-arm push	K	Two children sit on floor, soles of feet touching. One child has knees bent; pushes both his feet against other child's feet, who bends knees as first child straightens his. Repeat, using arms. Move feet or arms alternately instead of both together.	

Skill	Activity	Modality	Procedure	Code
B. Laterality (contd.)	5. Run in place	K	Put palms of hands on floor; one foot stretched back other knee bent. Without moving hands, jump to alternate the foot stretched back. Do rapidly.	
	6. Stepping stones	K V	Place red elastic on right ankle, green on left. Place cut-out red and green footprints on floor in desired pattern. Child walks or hops, placing right foot on red footprint and left foot on green. Adjust the pattern to control the difficulty.	
	7. Rope jumping	K	Usual procedure: both feet, alternating feet.	II B 7
	8. Swimming	K	Do with trained instructor.	
	9. Riding tricycle	K	Usual procedure.	II B 9

III. FINE MOTOR COORDINATION

Skill	Activity	Modalit	Procedure	Code
A. Hand control and Tactile activities	1. Paper punch	K	Punch holes in paper.	
	2. Use spring clothespins	K	Clip to top of a box; hang up clothes on clothesline, etc.	

Skill	Activity	Modality	Procedure	Code
A. Hand control and Tactile activities (contd.)	3. Clay; play dough	K T	Free play; make objects; make shapes.	
	4. Soap flake modeling	K T	Free modeling; make objects; use for tactile pictures.	
	5. Finger plays	K V K A	Usual procedure.	III A 5
	6. Tearing paper	K V	Make torn paper pictures.	III A 6
	7. Buttoning; zipping tying	K V	Usual procedures.	III A 7
B. Eye-hand coordination	1. Tinker toys, Lincoln logs, etc	K V	Usual procedures.	✸
	2. Stringing objects	K V	String beads, cheerios, macaroni.	III B 2
	3. Sewing cards	K V	Usual procedures.	✸
	4. Coloring, painting	K V	Usual procedures.	✸
	5. Cutting, pasting	K V	Usual procedures.	✸
	6. Ring toss	K V	Throw a ring over a peg.	■
	7. Drop clothespins into jar	K V	Usual procedures.	■

Skill	Activity	Modality	Procedure	Code
B. Eye-hand coordination (contd.)	8. Pegboards	K V	Free use; reproduce a teacher-made 3-D model; reproduce a design from a printed pattern.	III B 8
	9. Blocks	K V	Piling, building.	✸
	10. Trace stencils, templates; trace around objects	K V	Usual procedures.	✸
	11. Trace dotted line patterns	K V	Usual procedures.	III B 11
	12. Ball play balloon play	K V	Rolling, kicking, tossing, bouncing, catching.	III B 12
	13. Bean bag toss	K V	Use cut-out clorox bottle for catching bean bag.	■

IV. FORM PERCEPTION

Skill	Activity	Modality	Procedure	Code
A. Matching shapes	1. Walk around form	K V	Child walks around form on floor (made with tape, rope, etc.)	✸
	2. Match blocks	K	Blindfolded, child feels of one stimulus block; then finds one like it among other blocks.	■
		K V	Teacher shows picture of shape; child finds block like it.	

Skill	Activity	Modality	Procedure	Code
A. Matching shapes (contd.)	3. Sort blocks	K V	Sort blocks by shape.	✳
	4. Form boards	K V	Usual procedures.	✳
	5. Tracing on child	K T V	Teacher traces a shape on child's back with her finger; child finds a block of the same shape.	✳
			Same as above, except child finds a picture of that shape.	■
	6. Shapes Lotto® 30	V T	Spin for visual stimulus; match shape on board visually or tactually.	IV A 6
	7. Worksheets	V	Mark shapes that are like a key shape.	IV A 7
B. Construct shapes	1. Make large shapes on floor	K V	Use ropes, blocks, tape, etc.	✳
	2. Make shapes using various media	K V	Join straws together with large pipe cleaners to make shapes.	✳
		K V	Make solid shapes of clay, or flour and salt dough. Use cookie cutters to cut shapes. Use strings of clay to form outline of shapes.	✳

Skill	Activity	Modality	Procedure	Code
B. Construct shapes (contd.)	3. Use shapes for a picture	V	Assemble and paste pre-cut basic shapes to make a picture.	IV B 3
	4. Make shapes on a pegboard	K V	Construct basic shapes.	
		K V	Construct shape when given a model or 3-D stimulus.	■
			Construct shape when given a visual stimulus.	✴
	5. Make shapes on a geoboard with rubber bands	K V	Same as for pegboards, #4 above; *see* B5 for directions for making a geoboard.	✴
C. Reproduce shapes	1. Template tracing	K T V	Trace around shape of template: on chalkboard, on paper, in wet sand. Then reproduce from memory.	■
	2. Trace over shapes	K V	Place paper cut-outs under newsprint; child colors randomly on newsprint to bring out shape.	
	3. Shape pictures	K V	Make pictures out of basic shapes by tracing blocks or templates and adding other details.	■

V. AUDITORY SKILLS

Skill	Activity	Modality	Procedure	Code
A. Gross auditory	1. Identify sounds in environment	A	Child listens discriminatingly to sounds in environment. Sounds must be meaningful to that child: flushing toilet, dial telephone, horn blowing, typewriters in office, cash register in supermarket, etc.	
	2. Identify animal sounds	A	Take trips to a farm, animal shelter, zoo. Make use of every opportunity to listen to pets or other animals brought to school.	
	3. Imitate animal sounds	A	Child supplies sounds in a story, or play games with a friend using animal sounds.	
	4. Use sound toys	K A	Use toys such as musical pull toys, wind up toys, etc.	
	5. Experiment with sounds	K A	Use drums, piano; also bang blocks, hit a stick on various surfaces; balloon play; squeaking, letting air out, popping.	
B. Fine auditory	1. Discriminating sounds in environment	A	Listen to decide if sounds are the same or different.	V B 1

Skill	Activity	Modality	Procedure	Code
B. Fine auditory (contd.)	2. Clapping a pattern	K A	Teacher claps a pattern; child imitates; can be done with feet, drumsticks, etc.	V B 2
	3. Identify direction of sound	A	Children close eyes; teacher rings a bell. Children point to direction sound came from.	—

VI. LANGUAGE SKILLS

Skill	Activity	Modality	Procedure	Code
A. Listening	1. Stories	V A	Usual procedures.	VI A 1
	2. Follow directions	A K	Usual procedures.	—
	3. Records	A	Usual procedures.	VI A 3
	4. Filmstrips	V A	Usual procedures.	✸
	5. Listening exercises with worksheets	A K	Child listens to taped or recorded exercise; responds as directed on a worksheet.	VI A 5
	6. Library story hours	V A	Usual procedures.	✸

Skill	Activity	Modality	Procedure	Code
B. Expressing	1. Show and tell	V A K T	Usual procedures.	VI B 1
	2. Tape own voice	K A	Usual procedures.	
	3. Tell about experiences/ideas	K A	Children have an experience; tell about it; tell in sequence.	
	4. Retell a story in sequence	K A	Usual procedures.	
	5. Tell a story from pictures	V K A	Usual procedures.	■
	6. Conversations	K A	Conversing with peers, adults; take every opportunity to promote conversation.	
	7. Peabody Language©27	V K A	Follow information for the program.	VI B 7

VII. PRE-READING SKILLS

Skill	Activity	Modality	Procedure	Code
A. Auditory	1. Rhyme	A	Listen for spoken words that rhyme. Give a rhyming word for a spoken word.	■
		V A	Match pictures that rhyme.	

Skill	Activity	Modality	Procedure	Code
A. Auditory (contd.)	2. Discriminate beginning sounds	A	Listen to words to hear if they begin with the same sound.	VII A 2
		V A	Mark the pictures that begin with the same sound.	
	3. Sound-letter relationships	V A	Child finds the letter for a spoken beginning sound; finds all the pictures that begin with a given sound.	VII A 3
	4. Worksheets for beginning sounds	V A	Child draws line from letter to picture beginning with that letter; writes letter for beginning sound of picture.	VII A 3
B. Visual	1. Likenesses and differences	V K	Mark the pictures that are like a given picture; or mark the one that is not like the others.	VII B 1
	2. Classify pictures	V	Usual procedures.	VII B 2
	3. Arrange pictures in sequence	V	Usual procedures.	■
	4. Identify letter names	V A	Usual procedures.	VII B 4
	5. Identify colors	V A	Usual procedures.	■
	6. Worksheets	V K	Coloring sheets, letter names sheets, cutting and pasting sheets.	VII B 6

Adjusted Activities for the Blind Child

Appendix B

I. *Body Image*

- A3* Another child may trace the blind child, but the blind child may not be able to trace around another child. Outline his form with sawdust and glue or with whipped soap flakes (*see* Appendix C, p. 59, for directions). Then the blind child will be able to do part of the cutting and most of the coloring. Coloring is important for the development of the use of the hands and arms; it becomes a kinesthetic-tactile task for him rather than a kinesthetic-visual task as for the sighted child. He can also trace tactually around his own form.

- A7 Teacher may make a form of a person, outlining each part with a tactile material (sawdust or other).

*The letter and numbers correspond to the listing of the activity in the *Activities* section on the preceding pages.

45

If the form is cut so that each large body part is a piece, the child can learn to assemble it.

Use a doll such as a small "teen-age" doll whose legs, arms, head snap off; child can take apart and put together.

II. GROSS MOTOR COORDINATION

- A5 The blind child can do animal walks the same as a sighted child if time is taken to teach the kinesthetic movements tactually, actually moving the child's limbs until he gets the pattern. He cannot learn by imitation, so he must be helped to learn it kinesthetically. The exercise for him becomes one of satisfying body movements rather than one of fun in imitation.

- A6 The blind child may have a very realistic fear of running because he cannot sense objects fast enough to avoid them. Running needs to be taught by first having the child walk through the space to feel the terrain and to be reassured that it is clear. Running down hill facilitates the faster steps in running. The teacher may need to take the child's hand and run with him until the movements are established.

- A7 Same procedure as A5.

- A8 Blind child will need auditory clues instead of visual for the game "Simon Says." This can be done using auditory clues for the whole class or done alone in a small social group with the blind child. Procedures are the same: "Put both hands up," or Simon Says, "Put both hands up."

- B1 When the blind child walks on the walking beam, supply an auditory target (bell, tape recorder), placing it several feet in front of and somewhat higher than the child's head. This will encourage him to keep his head up, thus promoting improved posture. It also will help him to focus on the target instead of the process of walking itself.

- B2 In doing "Angels-in-the-snow," use tactile clues. Touch each limb and say: "Move this arm and this leg."

   Use auditory clues. Say: "Move your right arm and left leg."

- B7 Tie a bell on the jumprope, or string several large beads in the middle of the rope to give auditory clues as the rope is swung.

- B9 Tricycle riding requires caution. Child needs safe and firm limits; needs to know areas in which he can ride safely and the cues by which he can recognize these limits. A safe "fence" may be made by any low objects that the tricycle wheel will hit, as long as the child rides cautiously enough so he will stop at the "fence."

Additional Gross Motor Activities for the Blind Child

Walking in a straight line

Without vision to focus on a point, the blind child may have difficulty walking in a straight line, without veering toward one side or the other. The following are some ways to help him learn to walk straight. Daily practice is recommended.

Place an auditory target (tape recorder, someone's voice) across the room and instruct the child to walk directly toward the sound. By focusing on the auditory target, the child will more readily achieve a relaxed, rhythmical gait.

Make a narrow path bounded by rug samples or other tactile material. The child walks on the floor between the rugs without touching the rugs. Width of the path may be decreased as the child gains proficiency. An auditory target may be used for a focus.

Make a path by stretching two ropes for boundaries at about the child's waist height.

Extend only one rope. Child trails one hand lightly on the rope as a guide for walking in a straight line. Caution is needed to insure that the child does not "lean" on the rope, as this will disrupt the symmetry of his walking.

Even more effective, the blind child holds a ring that has been put on the rope, sliding it along to guide him. This is less likely to result in the child "leaning"on the rope. A long cane may be used in place of the rope.

Refrigerator box to locate space *

Preparation: Cut a door that can be opened and closed. Cut one shape (about the height of the child's shoulder) on each of the other three sides, perhaps a square on one, a circle and triangle on the others. Cut these so they will open and close. If possible, fix the "roof" so it can be taken off for easier observation of the child's responses. This is all that should be done to the box to start with. More components may be added as the training progresses and the child has mastered these basic concepts.

Objectives: The child will be able to . . . .

Demonstrate a more developed sense of laterality.

Show improved ability in relating his own body to positions and directions in space around him through practice in a small, controlled area.

Show increased facility in the important preorientation and premobility skills.

Procedures: After the child has explored the box freely, start the actual training by giving directions such as: "Go into the box and close the door. What (shape) is in front of you? In

---

*Taken from procedures developed by Mr. William E. Berinati, Blind Work Association, Binghamton, New York.

back? Face the door. What is in front of you now? In back? Reach out one hand. What shape do you feel? Reach out the other hand. What shape?

Use the terms left and right at this point only if the child has a good working knowledge of these terms. Many kindergarten children do not. Otherwise, use tactile or other clues to indicate the hand.

The ways to use this box are limited only by the teacher's and the child's imagination. Some suggestions include:

Child puts his head out a shape as directed.

Child locates a given shape and closes its "door". Then goes on the outside of the box to find the shape from the outside.

Child walks around the outside, inside to gain a concept of its size.

Teacher taps on the outside of the box. Child locates the spot and imitates the pattern.

As training progresses, add other components to the box. Paste tactile cut-outs above, under, on the sides, of the shapes already cut out. Use materials that are smooth, rough, furry, etc. Give directions involving the relationships of these tactile materials to the cut out shapes. Place a chair in the box. Say: "Put the chair under the cut out square so its back is next to the square. Sit on the chair. What shape are you facing?"

Later, the child can be helped to transfer the concepts of space that he knows in the box to a larger, structured space such as a corner of the classroom, and from there to other spaces in his world.

The practice sessions should be conducted daily and structured so as to attain the objectives stated above. Other children may work with the blind child to enhance the learning and to encourage social interactions.

III. FINE MOTOR COORDINATION

- A5 Since he cannot imitate from the visual, he will need his fingers moved through the actions until he learns them. For some finger plays, auditory clues may be enough. This is a good exercise for finger dexterity.

- A6 Tearing paper will become a tactile, manipulative task, fun in itself and useful for developing finger strength and dexterity. Any finished picture will become an added bonus rather than the goal.

- A7 In learning to button, zip, and tie, the blind child will need more motivation, encouragement, and direct instruction than the sighted child and will probably learn these skills at a later age. To facilitate his learning, use very large buttons with loose buttonholes, long shoe laces, and mount these on frames that he can use in front of him instead of working on his own clothes at first. Decrease the size gradually, and finally transfer his skill to his own clothing. These frames can be made easily out of scraps.

- B1–5 These tasks become kinesthetic-tactile for the
- B8–10 blind child rather than kinesthetic-visual.

- B2 Large textured beads may be purchased from the American Printing House for the Blind. Using a tray helps to keep the materials organized and within reach. Special trays for the blind may be purchased or one like a cafeteria tray may be used.

- B8 Pegboards offer many useful learning tasks for the blind child.

  Use freely for fun and for finger dexterity.

  Use both hands in coordination, one hand to find the hole and the other to put the peg in.

Develop directionality by placing pegs in a straight row: vertically, horizontally, diagonally. Do this from auditory clues, then from tactile exploration of a teacher-made model.

Make basic shapes following the above procedures.

- B11 Raised line patterns for tracing dotted lines may be made on a screen board, constructed by attaching plain window screen to a board frame (about 12 inches by 12 inches). The paper is laid on the screen, and a ball point pen is used to make the raised line. Experimenting will show the amount of pressure necessary to make the desired line. When the paper is turned over, the raised outline can be easily followed. The blind child should trace with his finger, not a crayon, to increase tactile awareness. This is very versatile and useful in the regular classroom as some of the same papers used by sighted children can then be used by the blind child.

  A raised line kit may be purchased from the American Foundation for the Blind that is like a clipboard with acetate sheets. When written on with a special pen with quite a bit of pressure, this produces a pronounced raised line on the top side of the paper. It is especially good for on-the-spot illustrating.

- B12 Ball play develops ear/hand coordination in the blind child and offers many opportunities for social play. A bell may be attached, or one can be placed inside a rubber ball that is then vulcanized. Audible balls may also be purchased. If the child uses the ball in a confined area, such as a corner, he will be able to roll, bounce, kick, and then learn to retrieve it himself from auditory clues.

Additional Fine Motor Activities for the Blind Child

The blind child needs to train his fingers and hands to work as efficiently as possible because his tactile sense in one of the two primary avenues of learning and communication for him. With increased understanding of the needs of the blind child, the kindergarten teacher's own ingenuity will prove to be the best source of ideas for activities that will be appropriate and effective for that particular child. The following suggestions will serve as a starting place.

Finger Strength and Dexterity

Unwrap candy or crackers in individual cellophane wrappers.

Squeeze the water out of sponges or cloths.

Use a typewriter, toy cash register.

Dial a telephone.

Screw tops on jars.

Use nuts/bolts, screws/screwdrivers, door latches, padlocks.

Spread butter on bread.

Pour from one container to another.

Stretch rubber bands.

Tactile Activities

Sort pieces of material of varying textures into a given category: two that are alike, the ones that are smooth, the ones that are furry, etc.

Make collages using a variety of materials with interesting textures.

Have many opportunities to feel animals, pets, farm animals, grasshoppers, caterpillar walking on his hand, ants crawling, worms.

Walk barefoot on many surfaces: grass, rug, warm pavement, wet pavement, wet grass, mud, stones.

Use a "feel" box for identifying objects by touch only. A "feel" box is made by cutting a round hole, large enough for the child to get his hand in easily, on one side of a small carton. If a felt flap is glued over the hole, this can be used with sighted children also. Each day place a different object in the box, one that has an identifying shape or texture and that is within the experience of the child. He is to put his hand in the box and try to identify the object. At the end of the day the object may be taken out and shown. Objects selected might be: small stuffed toy, apple, pineapple, balloon, orange. Sighted children may be hesitant to feel of the unknown, and this can be an excellent opportunity to relate this to the feelings of the blind child.

Sand play: modeling wet sand, tracing in sand, just enjoying the feel of it, pouring it.

IV. FORM PERCEPTION

- A1   These tasks with forms become kinesthetic-tactile
- A3—5   tasks for the blind child rather than kinesthetic-visual.

- A6   Shapes Lotto, as well as some other commercial games, may be adapted for use by the blind child. Raised outlines of the shapes on the spinner and on the cards will make this a totally tactile game. Sawdust and glue (*see* Appendix C) is one effective way of making a raised outline.

- A7   Worksheets for matching shapes may be made for the blind child by using the screen board (*see* Appendix C) or the raised line drawing kit (*see* Appendix C). It is important that the material on the page be organized in an orderly manner so the child will learn organization and a left-right movement.

- B1—2   These tasks in form construction become kines-
- B4—5   thetic-tactile rather than kinesthetic-visual.

- B3   The shapes for assembling a picture should be cut out of heavy material such as cardboard. Identifying the shapes and pasting itself can be a satisfying task for the blind child, with the finished picture of secondary importance.

- B5 A geoboard may be made with an 8 or 10 inch square board in which round-headed nails are pounded in ten rows of ten nails each. The nails should extend about one half inch. Use suction cups on the bottom or some other method to hold the board securely in place. The child stretches rubber bands across the nails to form shapes or patterns. This is a good way to develop finger strength and finger dexterity as well as shape perception.

- C1 Template tracing becomes a kinesthetic-tactile task rather than a kinesthetic-tactile-visual task.

Additional Form Perception Activities for the Blind Child

Two books are available for blind children that will help develop form perception by discriminating and identifying shapes made with Braille dots. The scope of the books is somewhat limited as only three shapes are used: the circle, square, triangle; these are always represented only in the dot texture. Various sizes of these shapes are used. However, much benefit can be derived by the use of these books:

> *Touch and Tell*© Cost: $5.75
> *Kansas Braille Reading-Readiness Book*© Book II.
> Cost: $2.20 for the child's Braille book
>   .40 for the ink print manual

These books are both available from the American Printing House for the Blind. They are very similar; purchasing both would be unnecessary.

V. AUDITORY SKILLS

- B1 Most of the activities to develop fine auditory discrimination will not need to be adjusted per se for the blind child, but will need to be done much more frequently and much more intensively than for the sighted child. He will need much more practice to gain proficiency in identifying at an early age the subtle differences in sounds, differences that the sighted child learns at a later age. Games and activities to develop the following skills will be helpful:

- Ability to identify a familiar person by his footsteps; to identify a person by his voice.

  Ability to identify which person of the several present is speaking.

- Ability to use environmental sounds to orient himself and to locate directions in space: the differences in sound when passing an open or closed door; the change in sound as it recedes; the sound of the flow of traffic in the streets; the sound of one's own steps when near a building or obstruction as different from in the open.

- Ability to discriminate various voice intonations reflecting emotions or emphasis of the speaker.

- Ability to associate sounds with the activities going on around him, such as a cake being stirred, running water, pages in a book being turned, the click of knitting needles.

B2   In addition to the usual procedures in clapping a pattern, a challenging variation is to use a Morse Code approach. A buzzer is needed, such as a doorbell, a buzzer on some walkie-talkies, or a purchased one. Make a set of cards with dots and dashes using sawdust and glue. Start with easy patterns (two dots; one dot and one dash) and gradually increase the difficulty to four or five dots and dashes. The child feels of the pattern from left to right and then reproduces the dot-dash pattern on the buzzer. This activity develops concentration and tactile awareness as well as auditory discrimination.

VI. LANGUAGE SKILLS

- A1 Many stories today are highly dependent for understanding and enjoyment on elaborate or eye-catching illustrations. It is important for the blind child that he have the opportunity to hear stories that are not so dependent on illustrations. Mother Goose rhymes, passed down orally from generation to generation, have a strong auditory appeal and lend themselves to oral telling, as well as having the added interest of rhythm. Traditional folk tales, such as Peter Rabbit and Jack and the Beanstalk, also passed down through storytelling, convey the story through words alone, with many repetitions of key phrases adding to the auditory appeal. Storybooks commonly used in primary classrooms will need to be analyzed carefully to determine their relevance for the blind child. Although the use of these books is not harmful to the blind child, they very well may not fill any of his needs at all. Care must be taken that the time spent on stories that are inappropriate for the blind child does not restrict his time available for using materials more suitable to his own language needs.

- A3 Story records need to be selected using the same criteria as above.

- A5 Listening exercises with worksheets may possibly be adapted for use with a blind child, but it is questionable that the benefits would warrant it. The time needed for the blind child to respond to the taped directions would be necessarily longer, and so the tapes would need to be remade to accommodate this. Other means of presenting the same learnings would probably be more appropriate in most cases.

- B1   Share and tell is an excellent way to broaden the experiences of the blind child as well as the sighted, as long as ample opportunities for detailed tactile exploration are provided for the blind child.

- B7   Many of the Peabody Language Kit activities will be appropriate for the blind child. Adaptations of the exercises involving pictures may include use of real objects or some tactile pictures. The oral activities and stories can make a real contribution to the language and auditory development of the blind child.

VII. PRE-READING SKILLS

- A2   Small objects instead of pictures may be used for matching beginning sounds. Extra time should be spent on oral matching of sounds.

- A3   Activities involving identifying letters and sound-letter relationships will need to be done under the direction of a specialist in teaching Braille.

- A4   The blind child can match letter cards to small objects beginning with that sound.

- B1   Two readiness books for the blind are available which help the child learn likenesses and differences: *Touch and Tell* and *Kansas Braille Reading-Readiness Book.* Both are available from the American Printing House for the Blind.
       The teacher will also be able to devise many similar activities using tactile pictures, shapes or real objects.

- B2   The blind child should be offered many opportunities to classify tactile materials and real objects and to classify words presented orally.

- B4 Learning to identify letter names will need to be done under the direction of a specialist in teaching Braille.

- B6 The blind child can learn to mark some kind of worksheets with a crayon so a sighted teacher can correct them. Sheets for matching letters, matching words, finding likenesses and differences are possibilities that might be used in this way.

Recipes for Tactile Materials

Soap Flake Modeling

With an electric mixer, whip one cup Ivory Flakes® and one-half cup water into a creamy consistency. This mixture may be applied with the fingers to fill in a stencil, outline a figure, and to create interesting tactile pictures by using a tracing wheel or other instruments to change the texture. If the soap mixture is mixed thin enough, it can be used to paint with a brush or to fingerpaint with. If mixed thicker, it makes a novel modeling material which will harden for permanent models. Dry powder paint may be added before mixing to make various colors that will appeal to the sighted children, thus promoting a satisfying social play situation.

SAWDUST AND GLUE

Use Elmer's Glue® (or similar) to outline the picture,

shape, or design that you want to have a tactile outline. Then, completely cover the glue outline with a thick coating of sawdust and pat down gently. Use lots of sawdust as the excess will shake off. Shake off the excess sawdust and let dry overnight. The sawdust will give a raised outline that is rough and easily discernible. This is a practical way to adapt a regular worksheet, such as a coloring sheet, that is used by all the children in the classroom to become a tactile sheet for the blind child. This can be used easily and successfully for making sets of cards for matching shapes, for cards with number sets, for making simple worksheets for likenesses and differences, etc.

SALT-FLOUR DOUGH (nonhardening)

Mix two cups of flour with one-half cup salt. Mix with enough water to make a clay-like consistency. Add vegetable coloring if desired. This can be used indefinitely. The dough may be used for modeling, rolling, outlining, strengthening fingers, and just plain fun.

SAWDUST MODELING

Mix five or six parts sawdust to one part dry wheat paste. Add water and make into modeling consistency. Sawdust should not be too coarse, and objects modeled cannot be made too bulky. Sawdust can be sifted in flour sifter to take out the splinters. Dry the objects as quickly as possible. Objects may be painted with tempera paint.

GLUED STRING FOR A LINE

Mix one part Elmer's Glue (or similar) with three parts water. Wind cotton yarn or string around two fingers and poke the string into a jar filled with the glue mixture. Make a small hole in the jar lid big enough to pull the yarn through. Squeeze out glue as yarn is taken from the jar. Use the string or yarn to form lines for pictures or forms.

Equipment for the Blind Child in Kindergarten

Special Equipment Needed

Braille slates and styli; Braillewriter

Raised line drawing devices: commercial or home-made screen board

Work-play tray to keep materials being used within reach: commercial or just an ordinary tray

Talking books
(If the child subscribes to these at home, regular story records and tapes should be used at school instead.)

STANDARD EQUIPMENT THAT SHOULD BE AVAILABLE

Tape recorder

Phonograph

Story records and tapes
(The same ones used for the sighted children are also appropriate for the blind.)

Variety of manipulative materials
(The same manipulative aids used for sighted children in the regular classroom are suitable for the blind child.)

SPECIAL SERVICES (OPTIONAL)

The blind child may be educated satisfactorily in kindergarten with no special services. However, the following two specialists can contribute valuable help and consultations:

An orientation and mobility specialist can give periodic consultation and guidance to the teacher in setting up and implementing training in motor and space skills.

A volunteer, certified in transcribing Braille, can make labels for the room, name cards, letter cards, transcribe experience charts, whatever else the teacher may need.

Sources of Help and Information for Teachers of Visually Impaired Children

American Foundation for the Blind, Inc.
15 West Sixteenth Street
New York, New York 10011

This national organization is a clearing house for information relating to blindness and blind persons. The Foundation concerns itself with research and publishes much free and inexpensive material concerning the blind. A listing of its publications and aids for the blind is available free upon request.

The Foundation also maintains the M.C. Migel Memorial Library, a free loan library of 30,000 items for people interested in the field of blindness. Four titles may be borrowed at one time for a period of one month. Photocopies of periodical articles are available at ten cents a page. Bibliographies in the areas of interest (education, rehabilitation, recreation, etc.) are sent on request. Inquiries can be made to:

> M.C. Migel Memorial Library
> American Foundation for the Blind, Inc.
> 15 West Sixteenth Street
> New York, New York 10011

American Printing House for the Blind, Inc.
1839 Frankfort Avenue
Louisville, Kentucky 40206

APH supplies educational materials for blind children in grades one through twelve. It publishes books, magazines, and other material in various media: Braille, Talking Books, large print, and Braille music. All of the commonly used text series in all subject areas are available in Braille, as well as the workbooks to accompany the texts, dictionaries, encyclopedias, high-interest, low-vocabulary books, and other supplementary materials. APH manufactures many educational aids for blind students. It conducts an annual survey of blind students. Catalogs are sent on request.

Blind Work Association

To obtain the address of the nearest office, contact your state commission for the blind. The Association offers many social services to parents of blind children, starting in the infant years, giving information on financial assistance and other help that is available. The Association may provide the services of an orientation and mobility specialist who will guide the program or give direct training in helping the blind person get around independently. It provides vocational guidance and training as well as workshop employment for some. The Association trains and coordinates the work of volunteers in transcribing Braille and performing other services for the blind. It functions as the local source of information and help for the blind, especially important in the rural areas. Although it does not involve itself in the field of education specifically, its services and its involvement in all areas of the needs of the blind are directly pertinent to the teachers who work with a blind child in the regular classroom in the public school.

Howe Press of Perkins School for the Blind
Watertown, Massachusetts 02172

The Howe Press manufactures specialized materials for the blind, such as slates, Braille writers, Math materials, Braille paper.

It also offers Braille Vision Books®, a new concept in children's books combining print and Braille. The story is written in ink-print with the Braille version superimposed on the same page. This enables the blind child to feel of the Braille characters while he listens to the story being read by a sighted parent or friend. As he enjoys sharing the story, he becomes aware that Braille characters represent words and meaning.

The Howe Press also produces Braille Fragrance Books®. These books have fragrance strips, which, when scratched, give off the fragrance of the tactile picture, e.g. pine trees, oranges, peanut butter, etc.

Library of Congress
Division for the Blind and Physically Handicapped
1291 Taylor Street
Washington, D. C. 20542

The Library of Congress provides free library service to persons who are unable to read or use standard printed material because of visual or physical impairment. Books and magazines in recorded form (talking books) or in Braille are delivered to eligible readers by postage-free mail and returned in the same manner. Specially designed phonographs and cassette players are also loaned free to persons borrowing talking books. A bimonthly review of new materials is sent to the users of the services so they can make selections. Certification for eligibility for these services must be signed by a doctor or other professional involved with the blind person. Certification for use of these materials by a person with learning disabilities from organic disfunction must be signed by a doctor of medicine.

Lions International
209 North Michigan Avenue
Chicago, Illinois 60601

The community-minded men in this organization give their major service toward helping the blind. Specific help is given to the blind individual through local Lions' Clubs.

Special Education Instructional
Materials Centers (SEIMC)

These centers, usually regionally located, are resource centers, offering materials for preview and for loan. They can also supply much important information on the various instructional materials. These centers usually have available on request a listing of their materials. Borrowing materials is a practical way to become familiar with new materials before purchasing and to determine if they are appropriate for a certain child. Borrowed materials can also fill a short-term need for a particular child. Information on where these centers are located is available from the State Education Department, from area colleges, or from Special Education departments in the local school.

State Education Departments
Division of Handicapped Children

Most State Education Departments have a division set up to deal specifically with the needs of handicapped children. This division can supply information on available services, funding, materials, and teacher training. It may publish free or inexpensive pamphlets giving useful and practical help to those involved with handicapped children.

Touch Aids
C. and E. Hrueger
1790 South Juniper Street
Escondido, California 92025

Touch Aids manufactures excellant games for young visually impaired and blind children suitable for playing either with sighted or visually impaired friends.

Appendix F

Suggested Readings for Teachers

Books

GUIDING THE DEVELOPMENT OF THE YOUNG VISUALLY HANDICAPPED

Doris Groves and Carolynn Griffith — Columbus: Ohio State University, 1965.

This pamphlet lists practical activities by age level that are appropriate for use with blind children from six months to ten years of age. Some categories included are: auditory, language, body image, tactual, and locomotion. Other useful reference information is also listed. This is a handy reference for the classroom teacher.

TEACHING MONTESSORI IN THE HOME

Elizabeth G. Hainstock — New York: Random House, 1968.

Intended for the parents of all children, the book is extremely useful for teachers working with a blind child. After a short discussion of the Montessori philosophy, which itself may be very adaptable to the blind, directions are given for making many materials for educating the senses. Measurements, diagrams, and patterns are included. The emphasis is on self-care, independence and development of the senses; all of which are important to the blind child.

THE VISUALLY IMPAIRED CHILD: Growth, Learning, Development, Infancy to School Age

Carol Halliday — Louisville: IMC/RMC American Printing House for the Blind, 1971.

The format of the book is an outline of the development stages of the "normal" child from infancy to school age, paralleled by comments to show the similarity or variations in the same stages for the blind child. Some areas included are gross motor, fine motor, emotional, social, self-help, language, and readiness for school. The book is very readable and information on a specific area can be readily located.

THE OPENING DOORS: My Child's First Eight Years Without Sight

Lois T. Henderson — New York: The John Day Company, 1954.

The mother of a child born blind relates the first eight years of his life. The child was born in the 1940's when knowledge, understanding, and help for parents was far more limited than today. The parent's heartbreak, struggles, and perseverence provide much insight into the many factors influencing the blind child's early years.

THE SLOW LEARNER IN THE CLASSROOM

Newell C. Kephart — Columbus: Charles E. Merrill Publishing Co., 1971.

This book is a classic in the field of motor and perceptual training for all children. Its emphasis on motor skills as a foundation for later learnings is very important for all blind children. The sequences for training are as appropriate for the blind as for the sighted, if the necessary adaptions are made for the lack of vision.

BLIND CHILDREN LEARN TO READ

Berthold Lowenfeld et al. — Springfield: Charles C Thomas, Publisher, 1969.

The comprehensive discussion in this book centers around factors involved in readiness and beginning reading. A detailed report is included on a study of first grade reading for blind children. This book is recommended as much for kindergarten teachers as for other primary teachers.

OUR BLIND CHILDREN: Growing and Learning with Them

Berthold Lowenfeld — Springfield: Charles C Thomas, Publisher, 1971.

Up-to-date information on the blind child is presented by an author who has done much writing in this field. This is probably one of the best sources for basic general information on the blind child.

CONCEPT DEVELOPMENT FOR VISUALLY HANDICAPPED CHILDREN

William T. Lydon and Loretta M. McGraw — New York: American Foundation for the Blind, 1973.

The authors advocate that basic skills necessary for later orientation and mobility training be incorporated into the child's educational program from kindergarten on. This book presents the rationale and detailed suggestions and sequences for teaching these skills from body image to finding the way around the classroom independently. Many definitions of terms are given, as well as the form for Cratty's test on body image. This is an excellent book for teachers.

ADAPTING MATERIALS FOR EDUCATING BLIND CHILDREN WITH SIGHTED CHILDREN

New York Education Department — New York: University of the State of New York, 1961.

Many ideas are described in both print and pictures for adapting materials commonly used in the primary classroom for use with the blind. This publication is helpful in itself, but also serves as a catalyst for the teacher to become creative in adapting other materials.

ELIZABETH

Sharon Ulrich — Ann Arbor: University of Michigan Press, 1972.

The mother of a congenital blind child traces her child's development during the first five years. The family situation appears ideal. Since the child was a subject in a university study, guidance and support from trained personnel was available. Two sections on various aspects of blindness in young children were written by a member of the university staff and are as relevant to teachers as to parents.

PERIODICALS

EDUCATION OF THE VISUALLY HANDICAPPED

Published by the Association for the Education of the Visually Handicapped
1604 Spruce Street, Philadelphia, Pennsylvania 19103

Published four times a year, this magazine, formerly called the International Journal for the Education of the Blind, contains up-to-date information and research reports on topics relating to education. As it is the only major publication dealing primarily with the education of the blind, most current research is reported.

THE NEW OUTLOOK FOR THE BLIND

Published by the American Foundation for the Blind
15 West Sixteenth Street, New York, New York 10011

This magazine contains articles of general interest on a variety of topics related to the blind. Most articles are not specifically related to education, but some deal with the early development of the blind child. Published monthly except July and August.

Periodical Articles

"Believing without seeing: teaching the blind child in a 'regular' kindergarten"
Pearl E. Tait — *Childhood Education*, March 1974, pp. 258-291.

The author speaks directly to the kindergarten teacher when she describes her own first experience of having a blind child in her 'regular' kindergarten. The suggestions given for adapting the regular activities are practical.

Definitions

Appendix G

Adventitious blindness
refers to blindness that occurred at some time after birth.

Blindisms
are the mannerisms often displayed by the blind, such as rocking, head rolling, kicking, etc.

Congenital blindness
refers to blindness since birth.

Directionality
is the projection of the internal laterality outward to objects in space.

Facial vision
is the ability of the blind person to perceive extremely close objects by seemingly feeling a change of sensation or feeling upon the face. This does not involve light or touch, but sounds that are almost imperceptible.

Haptics
refers to the tactile explorations that go beyond the simple qualities of passive tactual sensation.

Kinesthetic
> refers to the sensation received from the muscular movements of the body.

Laterality
> is the internal awareness of the two sides of the body and the ability to distinguish between the two sides of the body.

Legal blindness
> refers to the visual acuity that does not exceed 20/200 in the better eye even with the best correction possible; or to "tunnel vision" where the visual field is less than an angle of 20 degrees. These definitions are used to determine eligibility for financial aids and for income tax exemptions.

Mobility
> is the act of moving around in the environment; locomotion.

Orientation
> is the use of the remaining senses to establish one's position in the environment even without sight.

Peripatology
> is the science of getting around in the environment. It is synonymous with orientation and mobility.

Residual vision
> is any usable vision of a visually impaired person, ranging from light perception to enough vision to move around in certain situations or to read large print.

Tactile (tactual)
> is the skill involved in gathering information through

touch. In relation to learning for the blind, it often refers to active exploration to get meaning rather than merely the passive touching.

Trailing

is using the back of the fingers to follow lightly over a straight surface for orientation purposes.

Verbalisms

are the words that the blind use that, for them, cannot be experienced by the senses, such as foggy, green, rainbow.

Visual handicap

refers to the degree to which a person's visual impairment prevents him from doing the kinds of things he wishes to do. A visual impairment becomes a handicap only when the impaired person considers himself handicapped by it.

Visual impairment

refers to any degree of visual loss that interferes with the person's normal functioning and performance.

Bibliography
and
Index

Bibliography

1. Abel, Georgie Lee: *Concerning the Education of Blind Children.* New York, American Foundation for the Blind, 1959.
2. *Adapting Materials for Educating Blind Children with Sighted Children.* New York, University of the State of New York, 1961.
3. Cratty, Bryant J. and Sams, Theresa A.: *The Body Image of Blind Children.* New York, American Foundation for the Blind, 1968.
4. Dobecki, Paul R.: Verbalism and the blind: a critical review of the concept and the literature. *Exceptional Children, 32:* 8, 525-530, 1966.
5. *Facts About Blindness.* New York, American Foundation for the Blind, 1974.
6. Frostig, Marianne and Horne, David: *The Frostig Program for the Development of Visual Perception.* Chicago, Follett Publishing Co., 1964.
7. Groves, Doris and Griffith, Carolynn: *Guiding the Development of the Young Visually Handicapped – A Selected List of Activities.* Columbus, Ohio State Department of Education, 1965.
8. Hainstock, Elizabeth G.: *Teaching Montessori in the Home.* New York, Random House, 1965.
9. Halliday, Carol: *The Visually Impaired Child: Growth, Learning, Development, Infancy to School Age.* Louisville, IMC/RMC American Printing House for the Blind, 1971.
10. Hammil, Donald and Crandall, John M.: Implications of tactile-kinesthetic ability in visually handicapped children. *Education of*

Visually Handicapped, 1: 3, 65-68, 1969.

11. Hampshire, Barry E.: Tactile and visual reading. *New Outlook for the Blind, 69:* 4, 145-154, 1975.
12. Hartwell, Dickson: *Dogs Against Darkness: the Story of the Seeing Eye.* New York, Dodd, Mead, and Co., 1960.
13. Henderson, Lois T.: *The Opening Doors: My Child's First Eight Years Without Sight.* New York, the John Day Co., 1954.
14. *How Does A Blind Person Get Around?* New York, American Foundation for the Blind, 1973.
15. Kephart, Newell C.: *The Slow Learner in the Classroom.* Columbus, Charles E. Merrill Publishing Co., 1971.
16. Kissick, Patricia: Teacher orients visually handicapped on road to independence. *The Evening Press,* Binghamton, N. Y., June 20, 1974.
17. Kurshals, Ina W.: What is readiness for the blind child? *International Journal for the Education of the Blind, 8:* 3, 90-93, 1968.
18. Lairy, G.C. and Harrison-Covllo, A.: The blind child and his parents: congenital visual defect and the repercussion of family attitudes on the early development of the child. *Interpretation, 5:* 2-3, 157-186, 1971.
19. Lowenfeld, Berthold et al.: *Blind Children Learn to Read.* Springfield, Charles C Thomas, Publisher, 1969.
20. Lowenfeld, Berthold: *Our Blind Children: Growing and Learning with Them.* Springfield, Charles C Thomas, Publisher, 1971.
21. Lydon, William T. and McGraw, M. Loretta: *Concept Development for Visually Handicapped Children: a Resource Guide for Teachers and other Professionals Working in Educational Settings.* New York, American Foundation for the Blind, 1973.
22. Maxfield, Kathryn E. and Bucholz, Sandra: *A Social Maturity Scale for Blind Preschool Children.* New York, American Foundation for the Blind, 1957.
23. Middlewood, Esther L.: A child — though blind. *New Outlook for the Blind, 48:* 3, 61-65, 1954.
24. Mobility Training for the Visually Handicapped. Springfield, Visually Handicapped Services: Illinois Department of Children and Family Services, 1970.
25. Norris, Miriam: *The School Age Blind Child Project.* New York, American Foundation for the Blind, 1961.
26. Parrish, John L., and Chassen, Larry R.: Variables in tactual

perception. *Education of the Visually Handicapped, 4*: 8, 76-79, 1972.

27. Peabody Language Development Kit, Circle Pines, Minnesota, American Guidance Associates.

28. Rogow, Sally: Perceptual organization in blind children. *New Outlook for the Blind, 69:* 5, 226-233, 1975.

29. Saxe, John Godfrey: *The Blind Men and the Elephant.* New York, McGraw-Hill Book Co., 1963.

30. Shapes Lotto, Springfield, Massachusetts, Milton Bradley Co.

31. Stocker, Claudell S.: *Modern Methods of Teaching Braille Book I. Kansas Braille Reading-Readiness Book.* Louisville, American Printing House for the Blind, 1970.

32. Tait, Pearl E.: Believing without seeing: teaching the blind child in a "regular kindergarten". *Childhood Education, v. 50:* 3, 258-291, 1974.

33. Tupper, LaVerne: *Tips for Teachers Working with Visually Handicapped Children.* New York, Commission for the Blind: State Department of Social Welfare.

34. Ulrich, Sharon: *Elizabeth.* Ann Arbor, University of Michigan Press, 1972.

35. Curry, Genevieve I.: *Winter Haven's Perceptual Testing and Training Handbook.* Winter Haven, Fl., Lion's Research Foundation, 1969.

Index

A

Acceptance
  parental, 4
  teacher, 4
Activities
  adjusted for the blind, 45-58
  regular kindergarten, 31-44
American Foundation for the Blind,
    7, 51, 63
American Printing House for the
    Blind, 26, 50, 54, 57, 64
Audible ball, 51
Auditory skills
  activities for, 32, 41-42, 43-44, 46,
    47, 48, 49, 51, 54-56, 57
  development of, 9-10, 12, 15
  research, 9

B

Berinati, William E., 48
Bill of Rights for the Blind, ix
Blindisms, 17-18
  definition, 75
Blindness, xi-xii, xiii, xiv, 3-4, 14, 15,
    16
  adventitious, 3, 75
  congenital, 3, 8, 75
Blind Work Association, 64

Body image
  Activities for 33, 45, 48-49
  development, 6
  evaluating, 26
  orientation and, 21
Braille reading (*see also* Pre-reading
    skills)
  equipment, 61, 62, 64, 65, 66, 67
  letter names, 44, 57-58
  readiness for, 26, 54, 65
  volunteer, 62
Bucholz, Sandra, 14

C

Child development, xi-xii, xiii, xiv
Classroom teacher, xi, xiii-xiv, 6, 12,
    13, 18, 21-22, 23, 52
Concepts, development of, 10-11, 16,
    21, 82
Counseling, parental, 4
Cratty, Bryant J., 26

D

Development, early, 3-14, 81
Directionality
  activities for 48-49, 51
  definition, 75
  development of, 6, 19-20
  laterality and, 20

orientation and mobility and, 20
Dobecki, Paul R. 11
Doll, Edgar, 25

E

Ear-hand coordination, 5, 51
Education
  auditory skills in, 9-10
  implications of blindness on, 15-16
  philosophy, xiii, xiv
  public school, xiv
  rural areas, xii
  tactile skills in, 7-8
Equipment for blind child, 61-62, 63,
    64, 65
Evaluation
  body image, 26
  psychological, 27
  social skills, 25
  tactile skills, 26
Eye-hand coordination, activities,
    37-38
Eye poling, 17 (*see also* Mannerisms)

F

Facial vision, definition, 75
"Feel" box, 53
Fine motor coordination, activities,
    36-38 (*see also* Finger dexter-
    ity)
Finger dexterity, activities, 36-38,
    50-52
Form perception, activities, 38-40,
    48-49, 53-54
Frostig, Marianne, 8

G

Geoboard, 40, 54
Griffith, Carolynn, 13, 69
Groves, Doris 13, 69

H

Hampshire, Barry E., 8

Handicapped children
  classifying, xii
  labeling, xii
  mainstreaming, xi
  state aid, xii
Haptics, definition, 75
Harrison-Corvello, A., 9
Howe, Dr. Samuel Gridley, ii
Howe Press of Perkins School for the
    Blind, 65

I

Initial consonants, discriminating, 44,
    57

K

Kephart, Newell C., 8, 70
Kinesthetic
  activities for, 32, 33-44, 46-49, 51
  definition, 76
Kurzhals, Ina W., 14

L

Lairy, G. C., 9
Language skills
  activities for, 42-43, 56-57
  concepts and, 16
  concrete experience, 10-11
  development of, 9-12, 16
  research, 10-11
Laterality
  activities, 35-36, 48-49
  Braille reading and, 19
  definition, 18, 76
  development of, 6, 18-20
  directionality and, 20
  importance of, 19
  orientation and mobility and, 20
  posture and, 19
  reversals and, 19
  right and left and, 19
Learning
  early stimulation and, 3-4, 5, 7,
    9-10, 12, 14

imitation in, 6, 14, 15
implications of blindness in, 15-16
Legal blindness, definition, 76
Library of Congress, 66
Lions International, 66
Listening
  activities, 42, 56-57
  materials, 64, 65, 67
  Lowenfeld, Berthold, 71
Lydon, William T., 21, 71

M

Mainstreaming, xi
Maxfield, Kathryn E., 14
McGraw, M. Loretta, 21, 71
M. C. Migel Memorial Library, 64
Mobility
  activities for, 46-49
  definition, 76
  developing readiness for, 5, 6
  importance of, 20
  in the classroom, 21-22
  specialist, 20-21, 62, 65
  training in, 20-22, 82
Montessori materials, 69-70
Motor coordination (*see also* Kines-
    thetic, Mobility, *and* Orienta-
    tion)
  development, 5-6
  fine, activities for, 36-38, 50-53
  gross, activities for, 34-36, 46-49

O

Organization skills
  at home, 22
  at school, 23
  perceptual, 8, 83
Orientation
  definition, 76
  location in space, 48-49
  motor development and, 6
Orientation training
  in the classroom, 21-22
  specialist, 20-21, 62, 65
Overprotection, 18

P

Peabody Language Development Kit,
  43, 57
Pegboards, 40, 50-51
Peripatology, definition of, 76
Piaget, Jean, 8, 21
Posture, 6
Pre-reading skills, activities for,
  43-44, 57-58 (*see also* Braille
  reading)

R

Readiness books, 54, 57
Reading readiness, xi, 82
Readings for teachers, 69-73
Records, story, 42, 56, 64, 66 (*see
  also* Talking Books)
Refrigerator box
  training space in, 48
Rejection, 4
Residual vision, definition, 76
Rocking, 17
Rogow, Sally, 8, 9
Running, 34, 46

S

Self-care skills
  dressing, 13
  feeding, 13-14
  toilet training, 13
Shapes (*see* Form perception)
Shapes Lotto, 39, 53
Social development
  blindisms and, 17-18
  evaluating, 25
  in school, 12, 15
  peers, 12
  preschool, 12
  role of parents and teachers in,
    12-13
  stimulation of, 12-13
*Social Maturity Scale for Blind Pre-
  school Children,* 14, 25, 82
Sources of further information,
  63-67

Space
  activities, 46-49
  concepts of, 6
  organization, 21
Special classes
  benefits, educational, xii
  legality of, xii
  self image and, xii
Special Education Instructional Mate-
    rials Centers (SEIMC), 66-67
State Education Departments, xii,
    xiii, 67, 72, 81, 83
Stimulation, early (*see* Learning)

T

Tactile, definition, 76-77
Tactile materials (*see also* Special
    Education Instructional Mate-
    rials Centers)
  "feel" box, 53
  geoboard, directions, 54
  glued string, 60
  raised line kit, 51, 53, 61
  salt-flour dough, recipe, 60
  sawdust and glue, 45, 53, 55
    recipe, 59-60
  sawdust modeling, recipe, 60
  screen board, 51, 53, 61
  whipped soap flakes, 45
    recipe, 59
Tactile skills, 6-8

activities, 32, 33, 35-40, 45, 47,
    48-49, 50-51, 52, 53, 54,
    57-58
  research, 7-8, 81, 82-83
  training, 7, 8, 15
Talking Books, 61-62, 64, 65, 66
Teachers of the blind, certification
    of, xiii
Templates, 38, 40, 54
Tests
  Body-Image of Blind Children, 26
  psychological, 27
  *Social Maturity Scale for Blind Pre-
    school Children,* 25, 82
  Roughness Discrimination Test, 26
Touch Aids, 67
Training, definition, 77

V

Verbalisms
  definition, 11, 77
  research, 11
Visual activities, 32, 33, 34-40, 42-44
Visual impairment, 16
  definition, 77
Visual handicap, definition, 77

W

Walking, 47-48
Walking beam, 35, 46-47
World War II, xiii

Date Due

M